THE NECKLACE

Also by Florence Chard Dacey

The Swoon
Lightning (libretto)

THE NECKLACE

Florence Chard Dacey

Midwest Villages & Voices
Minneapolis

For valuable criticism and their help in preparing the manuscript I wish to thank especially Linda Curtler, Gayla W. Ellis, Kevin FitzPatrick, Pat Kaluza, Ethna McKiernan, Monica Ochtrup and Barton Sutter. Thanks also to Elizabeth Erickson, Susan McDonald and Maria Mazzara for creating the art for this book and to my parents, Pauline and Warren Chard, for their generous support of my work.

Acknowledgment is made to the following magazines in which some of these poems or earlier versions of them appeared: *Lake Street Review, Milkweed Chronicle, Nimrod, North Country Anvil, Poetry Now, Sing Heavenly Muse!* and *WARM Journal.* Several of these poems also appeared in *The Swoon,* Minnesota Writers' Publishing House, Kraken Press, 1979. "Necklace" was first published by Ox Head Press, 1985.

Midwest Villages & Voices
3220 Tenth Avenue South
Minneapolis, Minnesota 55407

In memory of my maternal grandmother
Florence Stella Squire Sutton, 1890-1936
and her daughter
Charlotte Mary Sutton O'Brien, 1911-1947
and my paternal grandmother
Lillian Mae Hutchinson Chard, 1880-1967

And dedicated to all the women
who have given me
life and strength

CONTENTS

III PIECES OF GOD

FAREWELL

I search
for the straight path
back to wind
that only enters
through tall grass
as if none of it happened —
woman's crazed forehead brought to a floor,
a child damming tears behind stalwart eyes,
a million words pinioned in one man's brain —

We will hide there
in that tall grass
inside the wind.

I am taking with me
the entire blameless world:
all the children, trees and rivers, motley cats.
Single file, still as thieves,
we pass you now.

See, their hands are your
forgotten soft gods,
their faces the shy moons
of your childhood,
each lost essential silence.

How we love you!

But we are leaving.

COMPOSTING

THOSE NIGHTS WE CHILDREN LAUGHED IN BED

We were an unconscious grove settled upon by a trilling migrant flock, five fountains for once perfectly synchronized, subcontinental plates heaving in our beds. We laughed room to room, across the black hall, the human-made barriers, five voices braced like an open hand against the movement under our beds, up against our eyeballs.

Now, that's enough, my mother would call, when she thought of it, from her light below yet above us always. Enough of what? For we didn't recall what set us off. A global pun we'd dreamed as one the night before? The joke the grown-ups shared repeatedly in their marriage beds? It didn't matter. We all laughed singly, together, shaking as we married each to each, mouths wide, sides aching, burying heads in pillows, laughing till it hurt, till we nearly cried,

for we knew at once the blood-truth that sprayed and made us be merry in tune, in time and out, let us be one, and how, years later, we'd be lying on our backs, grown-up and stiff in stocks and poems, children and silence, awaiting still that first step on the back stairs, by the father, home late, that meant we could yield with relief to a familiar fear, the voice that returned clocks and walls, that held our madness at bay, and hollowed in the dark a place for day.

FIRST MENSTRUATION

I should have known
from the way the *Life* magazines
with half-naked ladies disappeared
abruptly from our living room floor
things would not be easy.
Maybe so personal a matter
requires the impersonal,
a pamphlet from the leading
sanitary napkin manufacturer
with neat unstained drawings.
My mother hands me this printed truth,
an oblong wad of clean white rags,
somehow bound together,
two safety pins.
"We'll get you something
in the morning," she says,
her eyes on my shoulders.
She leaves before I can stammer
what I want to say:
Where do I put this?
It's three a.m. I'm thirteen,
standing in the upstairs hall
of an eighty-year-old house
on a lake near Chicago
in America
with a homemade
sanitary napkin
in my hand.

FOR AUSTIN
AT THE "PRE-SCHOOL ROUND-UP"

When my blood-and-water female push
sent you sliding down and out,
you were perfect.
You were.
Now the therapist tests your bite
and listens to your l's that sound like w's,
and you are nearsighted, the tests reveal.
I watch your hands pulling at your shirt,
your foot moving in a nervous arc.
I am weeping here at my kitchen sink, remembering,
because we have been found out, accused.
I fall, again and again, with you,
rage in my throat and lungs, each breath
a sweet suspicious pain.
You were not perfect, but you were.
You were not innocent, and yet,
sheltered from all this, you sheltered me.
I feel I have betrayed you with my very genes
and, worse, delivered you with a kiss
into the hands of such friendly strangers.

ROCKING

I am rocking Fay,
and someone is rocking us.
Her father and the boys are rocked too,
but the motion's not the same.
We two, we inherited
the same ache, atom-based.
Men fill us fine, but still . . .
And so I hold a child to breast,
not any child, but girl-child.
I mean no ill, but it's good to feel
life a little less inside, and more, at once.
Because this child is wombed, I lose and gain.
She is the mirror that tells me at last
there was never any mistake.
But now she only cares to drink and doze—
stuff for greeting cards, indeed.
Take our picture, advertise everything!
Mother's milk, baby's quilt,
Grandma's rocker, and don't forget
the human mouth,
the human breast,
the human sleep
love charges nothing for,
the softest sleep
we'll ever know.

FOR EMMETT, WHO IMAGINES WE ARE ROBBERS
DISGUISED AS HIS PARENTS

You sense
our plundering hearts,
the hidden empty pouch,
your own young gold.
You are the first safe
son. We lay our fingers
lightly on your head,
listening for the small inevitable
click, that opening into untouched riches.
Oh, the span of your cool vault!
There, we remove our masks
again and again,
parade as beasts or superfolk
or the shuffling sand creatures
of your dreams,
when we're not robbers.
But Emmett, not all our stealing
nor your mind's leaping, costuming us
against the certainty of the meager self
can stay that last disguise,
the impending gleam of bone.
So we reach into your brain
and say, as parents will:
We are all robbers.
We are all robbed.
The treasure flows around us,
our human greed the certain shoals.
When we walk the street together,
the unmistakable sound
of showering jewels.
In our beds, pearls.
In one hand, the knife.
In the other, love,
that inviolate stone
for which we die.

COMPOSTING

Throw in a little bit
of everything:
outer leaves of artichoke,
outrageous old potatoes,
young sparrows flung
by spring's caprice
to unceremonious death,
even heart and head
of unsuspecting gopher,
compliments of the cat,
and clippings of hair
dark and fair
from your three children's heads,
absurdly beautiful,
fashioned like fruits
of the gods,
knowing here
midway in your life
how everything moves
toward one fine heap,
one broken breathing
corpse of blood, brain,
husk and shell
which could,
if we only willed,
replenish this earth.

SHE COMFORTS A BLEEDING CHILD

The blood comes out. It will not stay.
It must flow away from us toward other.
No blood is lost, not birth blood
or the virgin's, not the soldier's or yours,
from some small wound or your spontaneous nose.

Perhaps there is a great pool of it somewhere,
hidden in our mother's eyes, turned royal and blue.
Or perhaps it is that place we drink at
in the dream, where even terror has its sweetness.
Or it might be we swim in it, blind and wet.

When you bleed, you bless. That's what it means,
though the stain upon your pillow, the trickle
from the dead man's lips seem not to fit that definition.
Still, taken alone, the blood is beautiful.
We drink it all our lives and do not cringe.

So when we stop that flow, as we always try,
we go against some old law, though not to stay it
goes against another. I think there is no end to loss,
even when I say what I am sure of, that no blood shall be lost.

I AM COOKING

Watch out! I am burning pans.
I am stirring up trouble
for your empty craw.
I am watching my life simmer
while I tear down herbs
from my drying past.
I chew on three obscene cloves
of garlic. No evil
will befall you.

Oh, my singed meat!
Oh, my bloody bones!

Here in my laboratory
I draw out juices.
My liver and kidneys will
tide you over to Jerusalem.
I stir with my heart, a claw.
My kitchen is a cauldron,
the giant's mouth.
Drop in. Here we
fritter, we stew, we
pickle, fry and render.

Oh, wild scalding in the kitchen!
Oh, thick spoons flying by the windows!

I am cooking here, not my mother.
My breasts are raw. Grease is spitting.
The floor's alive. It croaks and humps.
The table bulges like a mushroom.
My hands are plates. They multiply.
My head is dinner gong.
I strike, I sear
against my family's heat.

Oh, come in to eat, my loves!
Oh, come in to food, everyone!

COMES THE DAUGHTER

If your body is a temple,
candles flicker at some portals.
Human incense drifts
from out the silken pillars.
You're the temple, Fay,
and priestess too,
all curve of catholic flesh.
I'm the old woman who goes ahead
intoning the new litany:
Out of a hole
comes the daughter,
world riddled, honey-combed,
ancient chapel, newly frescoed,
filagree of skin and blood.
Holy!
You'll never block the sun.
Fresh filter for the father's pain,
wind makes you its whistle.
You're a waltzing sacred grave,
forever daring strangers
like your mother
to leap into
your bottomless
ever-darkening
hoop.

FAY'S SONGS

1
Bones are beautiful.
If you didn't have bones
you couldn't stand up
and you couldn't sit down.
If you didn't have bones
you'd be all mush.
Oh, bones, bones,
don't you break,
beauty,
beauty bones.

2
I have a baby
in my head,
but I can't have her
if she's in my head.
I love babies
in my head.

3
I like my husband
sometimes,
but we fight.
I say,
I'll stay home
and take care
of these kids.
You go to work.
Go, go,
go to work.
I can take care of
everything here.
Go to work,
go.

4
Mrs. Kleppe's dead.
She's in the ground.
She may be happy,
I don't know.
She's like the butterfly
in our street.
It's lying there
and the cars go by.
My dad and I,
we sing songs
when we sit
by Mrs. Kleppe,
songs that fly.

MARIGOLDS

She plucks marigolds
and scatters them in the dusk,
squandering her gold
as the child must.

I put down my book to watch.
The trails of ruffled sun lead nowhere
but to her hand, small enough
to plunge into your heart.

I shall not speak of waste,
of the long wait for bloom,
or of the eye for which
we hoard any trace of beauty.

I shall not speak,
even when the sidewalk yawns,
the petals light her hair,
unmistakable temptation
for some waning god.

Maidens in me stir
at the flickering
yellow prance.
Rising, I whirl
with Fay and flowers,

crushing, crushed,
the scent more pungent
than the grief we waft
to one another.

We ourselves
raise altar here
and merry sacrifice.
Our scintillating skin

a destiny. Hades beneath
our skimming sandals.
The flowers gasping fates

she cannot,
I will not
read but choose
to dance
among.

FINDERS/KEEPERS

We know where small things wander
that men and children call for:
keys, pen, shoe. Or cherish:
ring, letter, feather. We know
with our palms and foreheads
because we have touched all these things,
imaged them in particular places—
under the radiator, on the dryer,
behind the tape in the middle right hand
drawer of the cupboard by the back door.

We have needed to remember
when no one else can
where small things come to hide
because we have needed to remember
ourselves, women, disappeared among men and children.

So, when my mother finds
a cherished silver earring I lost
at her house, she calls me
right away on the phone,
oddly triumphant.
I think it is because she has
kept faith in her way
with the small lost truths of women:
that we are each a word
our grandmother, mother dared not say
but could not forget;
that women need one another like water
and what some men call god
nurses the world through our hands and eyes;
that we can find ourselves in any mess
because we are, each of us,
each the separate cherished daughter.

We shine in the mother's skull
till we are found.
We are carried in hands
that refuse to forget
the feel of all
that's small and human-bound.

PARTING

I crave no more babies,
I say, sucking on the lie,
swaggering off to write.
My back is stiff from birthing.
I am over-qualified for this job.
Mouthing it like a toddler,

Mother.

I'm nurturing art.
No more fingering booties in the attic.
No more flipping whole-wheat pancakes.
This last child may cry,
but she'll outlive me,
just as I rehearse to outlive

Mother, you.

You carried five of us, all grown now.
Yet you are still putting up love
in your kitchen on August nights.
Can't let it go to waste. Mother-love.
The vine we prune back, but won't uproot.
We think we won't survive the cutting.

Mother, you did.

A mother does. Makes loss a religion.
Watches her body walk away
without a backward glance,
serrated into two or six or ten.
That, or straps the children to her
till she is one misshapen lumbering beast,
hacking at herself in vain, but

Mother, you did not.

Or live as if you didn't. Don't
pry or whine. Keep your calculated distance,
like this I calculate and cultivate.
Is it anything but shield
against that truth,

Mother, you did not tell me.

That we must let life and death
flow out of us in them,
know they know to hold them
is to kill, to let them go is too,
and that our daughters will return to say

Mother, you did not tell me of this.

You did not tell me I would have to breathe lies:
You'll be fine. I'll be back soon.
You did not tell me of this flesh that would
sprout in mine like wheat, this flesh
I fatten for the scythe.
You did not tell me I would be
both flesh and scythe.

Oh, Mother, you did not tell me of this parting.

MAMMOGRAM

I have these breasts,
in between A and B cups,
which is to say, not big enough
for the movies, too big for high fashion.
My husband fancied them.
They have suckled three robust children,
but do not quite fill a god's hands.

The technician has me
position each in turn
on the cardboard.
They have to be just so.

The room is cold, my breasts
clinging to me for shelter.
I think of women friends
who are breastless now,
who bought time by the knife.

Little hills, your spurting is over.
Still, I need you for my sense
of off-balance symmetry,
as referent for my mothering time.

Let me hear those
old milky ballads,
inviting suck!

Soft weapon that thinks
it can conquer by succoring,
twins who grew up in the same house,
without a mother,
you adopted me
but dream of leaving.

Don't go yet.
Stay to lead me forward
into my own arms.

EVE

BEFORE, BEYOND

The garden began in her mind
long before anyone's face,
oh, long before
a man's dark need
hooked her.

What if she thought she loved?
The garden never doubted.
The garden had plans.
She called it sleep and compromise.
It laughed when her breasts dried up.
It sprawled into her eyes,
and people held out their emptied tongues.

Because the garden could talk.

She let it talk a long time
about the colors of nothing,
till the garden fell through
her womb like thunder,
haloed her ankles.

When her feet spidered in dirt
the garden drew her down
like the sky's final night.

UNDONE

My mother's fingers, fresh from practicing Liszt,
part her dark hair. Her mother is not yet a dying flame,
nor her only sister languishing from the unchecked growth.
Pliant, the three of them, their lives a plait
of music, French, a nebulous grace they aspired to.
The mirror sends back a girl's bed. The dark
long hair streams between the two, a bridge
of sorts between the places where she dreams.
Is this the promise then, to the one female not to be
undone? And where is the father now?

My mother takes her hair down
in front of the heavy wood-framed mirror
where her dead grandmother stood long before.
The thick grey tresses part and the parting multiplies.
She is smoothing her day, falling away,
the wedding bed, the fading light, all in the mirror.
Now she spreads her fiftieth year,
draws fire with her brush.
And where is my father now, when hair is undone?

My mother and I stand apart,
but our lives are braided tight,
her cheerful grey, my brooding brown.
We let our hair down by moonlight
for fathers, husbands, lost loves to ascend.
The mirror breaks as do our lives.
The fractured light pierces us, then fires the bed
where the males all sleep, their dreams undone.

IN THE EYE OF THE BEHOLDER

The eye has to do with light.
We can weigh the eye,
correct the vision,
but she wants a new set of eyes,
that aren't his.
Something happens to light
from her body that strikes
a mirror, or even doesn't,
something happens in between
its traveling from her breasts
or thigh or the genitals
to her retina. As if
the very air were male,
as if the cells of the lens
had cocks and muscles
she didn't know about
that could bend the light.
This is your body, this is his.
His or the his you imagined.
The light goes in, right to your brain.
You look at his body as he looks
at your body, as you look at your body,
as you look at her body,
as you look at any body.
The photographs, the paintings,
the movies.
You look at the buttocks,
the breasts, at the bellies.
You have no eyes.
There is a red bird in your dream
with a baleful eye.
You draw him and the eye
eats up half the page.
You start talking in your sleep.
"In my eye," you cry.
You want to split open your eye
and get to the bottom of all this,
watching yourself as you do it.

EVE

It wasn't the best apple,
and I didn't need that bite. Rather liked the way it swayed there,
   day after day.
Everything stayed then. That changelessness began to wear on me.
Still, I would have hung on, immobile, curious,
   except for that serpent, trailing the dark behind him.
I forget what he said, but the tone was very impressive.
For me, time entered when I moved. As if I had stepped
   out of myself and were about to pluck myself,
   suddenly so delicious. I felt a sudden severing
   in my head when it snapped; cracked, I felt,
   and apple was my comfort.
Of course Adam made a stink about it. Wished he'd done it first.
Because although all hell broke loose, I started it,
   not him. I stepped outside myself and made a space
   for death to stream on in.
And why? Faulty chemistry? In which case you can blame
   him, with his defective rib.
The serpent then? I don't think he existed except in my spine.
Maybe it was Adam's fingers playing on my back that stirred
   him, till he stretched up to my brain. That would mean
   fear moved me, not desire. But we knew neither then.

Now, it seems, knew nothing.
"And wasn't that a kind of death?" I shout when he reproaches me.
He says it's all in the mind. That's his problem.
Mine is how to make you see that apple as I did.
How to get you moving as I moved.
I could flash my breasts or hiss.
I could tempt you with such fruit!
But the truth is, there's only one apple,
and there is one apple for each of us.
Pluck yours, taste the curse of who we are,
then get the hell out of the garden.

ACCOMPLICE

Often enough before sleep
comes the dead child
who snatched your day,
that dry heel of bread.
A girl beyond bribes,
whose riven eyes ask:
Why can't you claim
the glory you strew
as you fell into the sky,
drank fire and lived?

Her eyes glisten
like your warm chains.

Will you remember,
then eat her,
that mercy?

But you lie
like a fog
in your bed,
so she will go on
poaching your small life.

Black eagles
that feed from her hands
have aeries
in each mother's
hunger.

CONCEPTION

I don't know how he got in
but one day Samuel Despair
showed up in my kitchen,
introduced himself, took off
his clothes, showed me his body
riddled with the self-inflicted wounds.
Raw red mouths, all over.
Naturally, I asked what I could do to help.
He said go to bed with him.
Not wanting a suicide right there in my kitchen
and being always drawn to wounded things,
I did.

I touched every one of those sores,
got blood and dead skin all over me.
He put his seed in me, through
that wound that never closes.
For that one moment, the wooden face
warmed to yearning gratefulness.
Afterwards, I wrapped him with this purple cloak
I keep for such occasions.
He slept.

Every scar forgot itself.
I think I wept.

In the morning,
it was the usual
"I'll be in touch."
I didn't know just how
until today, when I first felt
Despair's child flutter in me.
Even before that I'd decided
when Despair mates
with a woman like me
one of the possibilities
might be something
with wings.

THE DARK SISTER COMES UP THE BACK STAIRS

The dark sister I keep
beating inside my head
who wants to seduce each husband
never closes her legs
though she must have
when I yelled
and she backed down the steps.

Even though I am tired
of all these refugees
I move among, I try
to be human, ask,
"What do you want, anyway?"
This dark scared girl,
like all the rest,
says,
"A home."

So, I have a boarding house
going here:
one old lecher we lock up,
the actress,
that guy who keeps snakes,
a girl who claims she's a wounded deer,
the prince with his battered head,
and now, this mute sex-pot.

Imagine the conversations.
Imagine me trying
to keep it all going,
everyone reasonably happy.
Not knowing really
how it all happened.

And then those nights
when they all decide
to gather in the big room
where they've studded the walls
with shells and bones.

Sometimes I can't resist
the music.
I slip downstairs
and all their faces
lift,
so radiant
for a moment
that I go blind,
some old self
crowded out
by this host
of twisted joys.

WALTZ WITH ME, FRANKENSTEIN

He's sprawled on our living room rug, reading Plato.
Chunks of dead flesh stick to the birds in the muted oriental pattern.
There is a skunky smell. The spine recoils.
Still he tries to smile, to play the man.
But I know who he is.
He's been skulking round my slopes for weeks,
flinging his arms out in mine,
smashing the Waterford along with the Woolworth tumblers.
And I know what he wants:
acceptance like a thick salve,
and to thrust his iron tongue in me,
conceive a girl to love him.

I stall.
Waltz with me, Frankenstein, I girlishly implore.
Press those bulging stitches to my brow.
One...two...three...
In Vienna they swirl in old prom dresses,
but here we're both patched up,
and I've called the National Guard
to remove you from my life.

Poor Frankenstein, he doesn't hear. His ears are bad.
He wants to learn the two-step.
His rotting feet flit like birds.
His head lolls back.
He hums a country-western tune
and drowns out all the sirens.
The sergeant, monster-like himself, arrives.
I turn him away. False alarm!

"Who needs you, anyway," I want to sneer,
"with your civilized uniform and gun?
I've got the perfect monster slouching in my bedroom,
and we're about to trip the light-fantastic.
You'll see me in his arms
at all the small town dances,
a black rose in my hair,
his buzzard eyes fixed on me.
Pressed so close,
no one would ever dare cut in."

MY MOTHER AND I DANCE, NEW YEAR'S EVE

We are two high school girls, dateless,
her husband slow to dance these days,
my own five hundred miles away.
Music will be our secret suitor.
We rise for his sake.
I cling to her knotted ringed hands.
She wills with a smile
the arthritic legs to slide, to lift,
to startle age from out the thin-flowered dress,
as minnows, chicks, whatever darts in flight.
My mother moves.
I know only one
who will force her to her seat.
But tonight she is, by pluck, a girl,
even if at odds with the drifting flesh
that dooms, yet transmits,
the perishable graces
sixty years in garnering.

Elizabeth, Monica, Lillian, Stephanie, Fay
(the constant tune the air sustains
from your merely being!)
if my eyes register even once
that movement out,
away from
this quicksand *I*
and to
you, in your solitary stands
along the wall at this dance,
this soft defiance
of the empty floor,
it is
because,
see, my mother
with some strange courage
moves.

She dances
to her coffin
bright with jewels
and the ripe conviction
of who she is,
the old tunes
cracking hot
in her thinning veins,
me above her,
holding on.

OLD MEN

Remembrance
of old men, their fragrant language
so foreign —

Spaniard with the patched shirt
whom the family arranges outside the door
in the chair with caved-in seat, beneath the sun
which on the narrow crouched street marches.
He will follow it slowly on his knees, all day,
dragging the chair like a penance.
I pass this deliberate reckoning with humility.
On my way to everywhere, I pass.

Herb man transplanted to city each morning,
sorting the mountain thyme, chamomile, anise and tansey.
He perches at the market's edge,
his life arranged into carelessly exact bundles,
a remedy for each of my terrors.
Here reigns the quiet vendor of compassion,
yet I buy everything I do not need
with my small purse of familiar nouns.
I buy false pain, gulp it down unsteeped,
leave herbs for old women in black.

Man with eyes the essence of parched maize.
He makes tortillas on a small machine.
The heavy wafers wheel out of his hands,
his face warm with unwitting grief
at this unweighable giving.
And I order what will suffice us
for this day, but slip out at the sight
of those pliant fingers, binding up my bread.

Is it that
they were
a bouquet
my arms
ache for
the lack of?

That time
is just beaten petals
that must be abandoned,
the lines to blur, then blacken?

Or that the bloom that's male to me,
the father's bread,
the humble-
ness, the balm,
all I thought
I could not pluck
are more closely rooted
here
above my breast
my own
my
foreign
soil?

AND FORGET

In the beginning
she forgot numbers.
How many cups to a quart.
How many miles to Paris.
Food and travel simplified.

She tried ringing home for an hour one day,
murmured her way into five awkward families.

Then names.
A daughter transposed to a sister.
The salesman graced with the dead uncle's nickname.

History faded.
She forgot the places
for family births and deaths,
where she stashed money and old hates.

Seasons washed away.
She shoveled banks of sun,
arms wet from falling leaves.

Had she been going straight home
with all the safe answers
in every pocket?

Now every word, each step
is become the empty slate,
herself before numbers,
name or vows.
the woman beyond
appointments.

POEM TO EXORCISE FALSE SUFFERING

Come candles and mirrors, thick bells and wise goats!
Everything magic! Come body, old hymn,
and girl of my memory, scared, fat and haughty.
Gather round, clasp me, let's spring all the past.
Those men, heavy-lidded with each daughter's loss —
ashes and whirl! Away with your acres of graves!
And mothers, stiff herons that stalk a child's tears
like swift fish, the husband a shadow of reeds —
away! And you may have my cracked skull,
the shoes of this victim, the whips and the rack,
the priestess who preached only pain.
I have seared on my coals. I have lain with my knives,
fed on the heart splattered and coy,
leveled the self into each stranger's coffin.
No more.
Let us invoke the sprung lid, the splits, cracks and pinpoints,
the places of squirming and leaping, the narrow escape.
Bring the bell of you, goat of you, memory like magic.
We will squeeze through like vermin,
shimmy through like the rain.
We will churn through like wind.
We will make that space wider.

EPIPHANY

A daughter crosses the desert too,
seduces illusions with fine milky fists,
tongues the marrow like male poise,
when her brain empties of water.

You think there aren't snazzy tents out there?
Coal-haired Englishmen with swords at their hips?
Maybe wet roses on the wind?
Or just dawn, that galloping pull of children's blood, east?

But she creates the scent of her own water
that will snake between herself and each mirage.

Sand arches like a snow.
Air slips her into its pocket.
Sleep is the only drift.

Even when her palms shred
like scorched flowers,
and her eyes echo a different sun,
lips hammered soft by flame
can still say where
the hooded cool rode out to meet her,
who she drank
and why she came back
her hair a cloth of jungle,
the bleached heart shining
every impossible way.

PIECES OF GOD

PIECES OF GOD

Some great breath
we will not breathe
keeps trying to say itself
with hacked-off breasts,
hands and tongues.

It is not earth.
Earth gulps blood like water.

We could be this breath,
the pieces of god,
if we let the first blue,
the fire's ghostly scent,
some ripe face slice
wildly through our hearts.

We could stop some blades.

The horrible wants us
to listen
like children
at a keyhole
to the rending
inside us,
to scatter light
like the sad
dismembered angel.

It proclaims this
with the fragments
of humans
by the hour
in what is still
the only language
we will do anything
not to understand.

QUESTIONS TO A BODY

Hip-light, bone-bed,
where are you turning?

Worm-wall, tree's head,
why are you burning?

Breast-mound, crab hand,
what can you cover?

Fern-thigh, hot-crack,
may I be your lover?

Snake-hair, cradle-jaw,
what face do you sing?

Webbed heel, veined arch,
where do we begin?

Body sanguine,
close to sweet,

hapless body,
mind's first meat,

answer now!

SLOW BODY

Very early we want the body
to leap, and the body often does
lie like that, for the best of reasons,
for art, or health, or as a bribe to lure us
across to something more like death.

But really, the body loves to be slow,
slower than its own blood and water,
slower than its thoughts about itself
and what it ought to be able to do.

Even in the womb, the body
takes its own time, says:
Now.
Feed me right.
Leave me
alone.

The flesh wants to fall slowly
from a great spiralling tower,
to burn slowly against a night sky,
to fail magnificently to continue.

It does all this
with the wisdom of the blind woman
who has lived out her entire life
in one dense house of trust.

FAT

Fat is no corners to hide in,
boulders in a shallow lake,
the beached dead whale,
prey for the gulls.
Fat is the mirror can't take it all in,
too much for reflection.
Fat is the pomegranate,
the watermelon, too messy
for discerning taste.
It's November gourd, black with frost,
dried seeds inside like stilled tongues.
Fat has no feet, is slug.
Myopic, it miscalculates any opening.
Fat is all mouth,
the all-season furnace
that heats nothing.
Step on Fat and you
are swallowed by need.
Sit down with Fat,
go to bed with Fat,
and you never get up.
So, you ask,
what to do with Fat?
Look at it.
Gnaw on it.
Get it between your fingers.
Then write it.
Write blubbery poems
that sprawl off the page,
that gobble up audiences,
that loom like buddhas
and will not be moved,
remembering that god is Fat,
so fat he has breasts.
There is nothing
that cannot suck there.

MORE THAN ENOUGH

For years I wanted
hedges against some inner paucity:
more food than any body needed,
more crisp green paper to buy permission
to be alive and harmless for months on end,
more presents with wrapping grander than my skin.

And I hoarded all the dark things:
limp bouquets of sins,
the long trains of sorrows
we would-be martyrs must board with bright tears.

Now I want less:
ten minutes cocooned with my father in his pickup,
death a friendly hitchhiker in the back seat,
the single moment in my kitchen when
I barter with myself and no one loses,
the small dish of another summer,
my children around that feast,
a solitary word like "yes" to decorate
the emptiness we sometimes give to one another,

and less,
less of the dark.

I want to hear
there are fewer missiles than the less than one
needed to destroy anyone I love,
that the number of sins committed is insufficient
to distinguish between the saved and all the rest of us,
and, from those countries far off
and that one beneath our ribs,
news that in the massacres,
fewer men died than women,
and fewer women died than children,
and fewer children died than
rain or footprints, pebbles or shells.

"WHILE SHE WAS BEING INTERROGATED, SHE WITNESSED THE DISMEMBERMENT OF A YOUNG BOY"

Carolyn Forché, speaking of
events in El Salvador, 1982

Austin is ten.
His ritual is a jumpshot to get
the dirty underwear into the floor laundry chute,
then one sideways leap, feet together,
towards the north wall in the upstairs hall,
a quicksilver hand
put out to the other wall
for balance.
A grin.
Just to feel
a rush of air
across both soles at once
or maybe a leap
guarantees sweet dreams.

He sleeps well this night,
as usual,
with his ears,
fingers,
his sex,
every part of him
safe, except
in my imagination,

where
a child is pieced into
a sawed-off hole called life.
The unclenched hands,
the shy budding penis,
the summery limbs
plummet like sodden flowers,
splatter to sicken
every ground.

Outside, the night,
emptied of all ideologies,
sheathes its knife
and with me
weeps.

NECKLACE

Layer upon layer
of bone, bead,
wood and stone,
heavier than your body,
breathing, sinister,
raised
at great cost
from the cave below the tree,
as common as your life,
strung that tightly,
as large as a shroud.
When you put it on,
the hands of the dead
will brush your flesh.
In this necklace
you can go naked.
You need never speak
of connections,
but must dance them:
Be tooth and shell,
grow tail and hooves.
The necklace hides all,
except the head.
And the head knows
someone is stoning
a woman somewhere,
severing a man's tongue.
At great cost
the head is upheld,
holds the necklace,
the curse, the beauty,
the talisman
I dream I need.

AFTER THE ATTACK

For Rufina Amaya of Mozote, El Salvador

Rufina Amaya will always be
in the forest of felled bodies
looking for her four young children.
Her mouth is stuffed with death
and skewered shut.

Rufina Amaya will always be
dreaming of the last child's mouth
pressed into the grave of her breast.
Something like a starved dog
gnaws in her womb.

Rufina Amaya will always be
digging in the unclaimed wombs of men,
her eyes blind with the unclaimed power of women.

Where was it she lost
the shadowed wrists,
the brave ankles of her children?

And where are the winged brown backs,
the first snows of the eyes,
the wet violets that streamed
like music to their palms?

Oh, where are the small furred animals of their breath
that leapt, and leapt, and leapt, and leapt?

EAT, EAT, EAT

As we are buying
sugar-spun purple mummies
in Guanajuato,
death passes by,

a meager trail of
tiny white coffin
the father bears

and knot of children,
slow thread of women,
great sprays of white flowers
needled in their breasts.

Up to the cemetery,
high up to the mummy factory.

Will we see this little one
in twenty years, flesh etched to bone,
bones robed in white
with the original hair
on display in the glass case?

Our children are eating
candy mummies with raisin eyes.
Eat, eat, eat!
Grow plump and immortal.
Fashion yourselves new skins
that the lime of these hills
cannot penetrate.
So when she plucks you,
death will have to open your skin
with flame.

Emptied, you will rise
like the fragile paper balloons
released before the church
at each grand fiesta,

red and green,
wider than the circle
of any father's arms,
thinnest paper on thinner wire,
a fuel soaked bell attached below.

Ringing fire
they head straight
up into the night
in a mindless dead-certain path.

Where?

To moon, river, empty field.

At their passing,
all the people in the square
lift their faces.

Florence Chard Dacey was born in Illinois and has degrees from St. Louis and Stanford Universities. She works as a writer-in-residence in Minnesota elementary and secondary schools, as well as doing other writing and teaching jobs. She lives in Cottonwood, Minnesota, not far from the Yellow Medicine River, with her three children.